KARA the KĀKĀPŌ

DANNI RAE ILLUSTRATED BY EVAN HEASMAN

Every day, Kara would look to the sky,
Watching all the beautiful birds go by,

But, no matter how hard she would try,
Kara the Kākāpō could not fly!

She could FLAP
and FLAP and
FLAP her wings,

She could JUMP and HOP

and TWIST and SPIN,

But, no matter how hard
she would try,
Kara the Kākāpō
could not FLY!

All of her friends would come over to play,
"Just give up, Kara, it's hopeless," they'd say.

But Kara knew there was
more than one way to fly,

And birds weren't the only things with wings in the sky!

So, she explored and she searched,
she wrote and she read,
About all of the other things
that could fly instead.

Until the big day finally came,
When Kara the Kākāpō built her very own PLANE!

Now every day Kara looks to the sky,
Watching all the beautiful birds go by,

Then she jumps in her plane,
straps her helmet on tight,
And flies through the clouds
from dusk to daylight.

She SPINS and FLIPS
and ROLLS and DIVES,

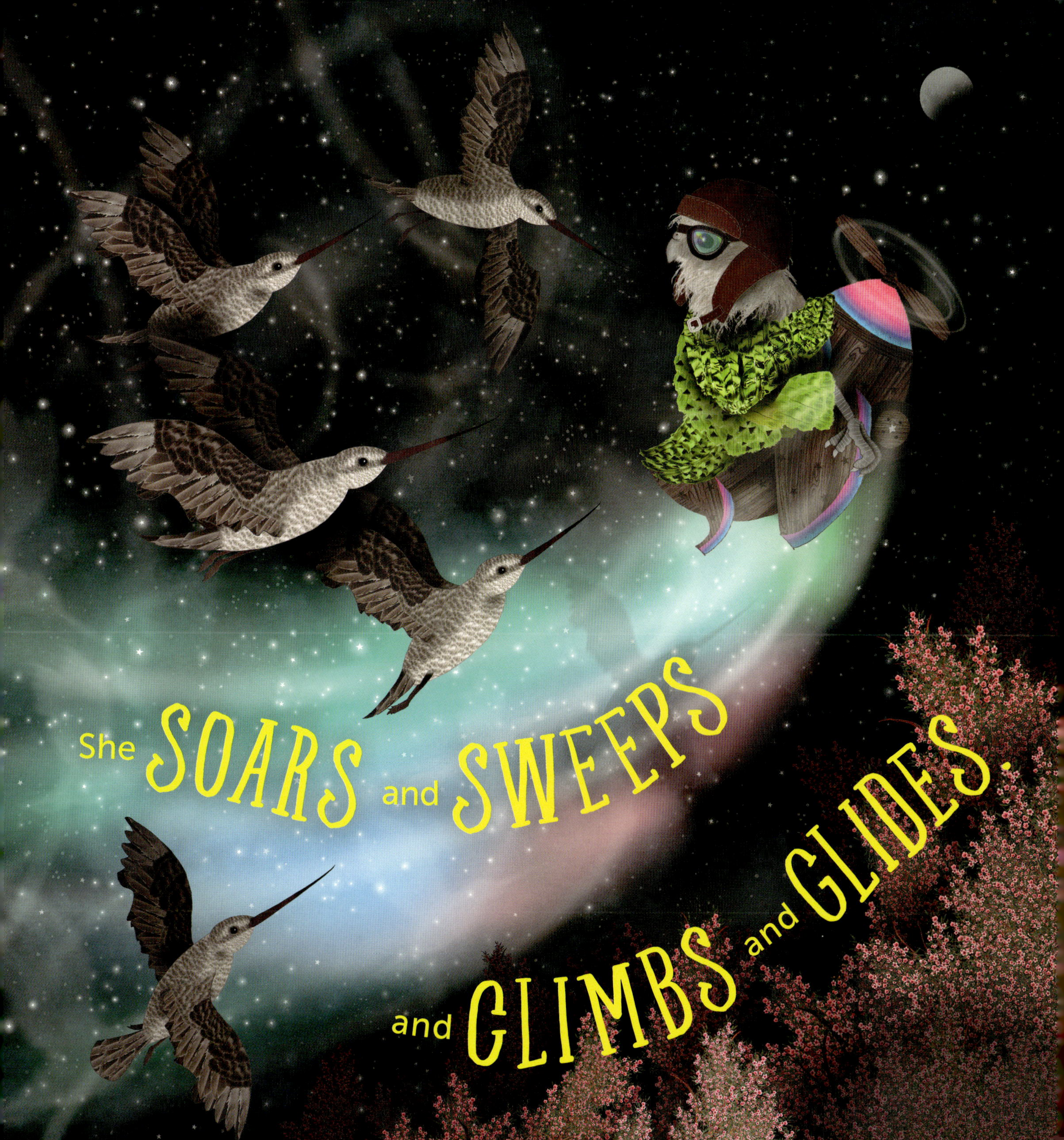
She SOARS and SWEEPS
and CLIMBS and GLIDES.

Because it does not matter
what others may say,
If you're willing to try
there is always a way!

ALL ABOUT KĀKĀPŌ

Kākāpō is pronounced Car-car-paw

WHAT AM I? I am a bird.

WHAT DO I EAT? I eat fruits, seeds and leaves. This makes me a herbivore!

WHERE DO I LIVE? I live in the forest.

HOW LONG DO I LIVE? I live for up to 90 years.

WHAT IS MY CONSERVATION STATUS? I am Critically Endangered (extremely high risk of extinction in the wild).

WHAT ARE MY MAIN THREATS? Mostly predators (introduced species like cats, rats, ferrets and stoats).

INTERESTING KĀKĀPŌ FACTS:

Kākāpō are the only parrot in the world that cannot fly

Kākāpō are only found in New Zealand

Kākāpō are also known as the 'night parrot'

Kākāpō are nocturnal (they sleep during the day and are active at night)

[Photo by Megan Jolly with permission from the Kākāpō Recovery Team]

DANNI RAE is a zookeeper and conservationist with a passion for connecting children with animals and the environment.

She has worked in Australia, New Zealand and Madagascar and wants to use her experience to inspire conservation connections through her engaging and educational animal adventure stories.

When she isn't working, Danni can be found writing, reading, hiking and travelling!

EVAN HEASMAN (also known by the artist name Soju Shots) is an illustrator who takes great inspiration from nature and fairytales.

He uses a combination of pen, watercolour, photography and digital mediums to create his characters and the magical worlds they come from.

He works between his home in beautiful Waipu and his little studio in Whangarei.

Published by Little Love, an imprint of Mary Egan Publishing
www.maryegan.co.nz

Designed by Anna Egan-Reid
Produced by Mary Egan Publishing

Printed in China

ISBN 978-0-473-62175-9